POWERFUL WORDS

Speaking God's Truth To Empower Our Lives

LISA HUGHES

WestBow Press books may be ordered through booksellers or by contacting:

WestBow Press
A Division of Thomas Nelson & Zondervan
1663 Liberty Drive
Bloomington, IN 47403
www.westbowpress.com
844-714-3454

Because of the dynamic nature of the Internet, any web addresses or links contained in this book may have changed since publication and may no longer be valid. The views expressed in this work are solely those of the author and do not necessarily reflect the views of the publisher, and the publisher hereby disclaims any responsibility for them.

Any people depicted in stock imagery provided by Getty Images are models, and such images are being used for illustrative purposes only. Certain stock imagery © Getty Images.

ISBN: 978-1-6642-0668-7 (sc)
ISBN: 978-1-6642-0669-4 (e)

Library of Congress Control Number: 2020918497

Print information available on the last page.

WestBow Press rev. date: 12/01/2020

WESTBOW
PRESS®
A DIVISION OF THOMAS NELSON
& ZONDERVAN

POWERFUL WORDS

WEEK ONE

Let's begin our study of powerful words with some facts on everyday words, the oxford dictionary contains 171,476 words in current use. Most native speaking adults know between 20,000 -35,000 words and the average four year old knows 5,000. In conversation, the average person speaks about 110-150 words per minute. Why tell you all these little statistics, because with all these word choices we have to be careful with the words we select and deliberate with the intentions of our words. Our words count! Read Proverbs 18:21 and write it below.

_____

_____

_____

What two things does our tongue have the power to bring _____ and _____. That is a powerful statement, we have the ability with our words alone to bring spiritual life or spiritual death to ourselves, others and even our circumstances.

The message translation says it like this, "words kill, words give life, they're either poison or fruit-you choose."

I want to bear good fruit in my life and I'm sure you do too and this tells us a good way to bear good fruit is to use life giving words. So where do we find these life-giving words? In the living word of the bible. The KJV bible contains 783,137 words. Bible Gateway suggests that there are as many as 5,467 divine promises in scripture, many have been fulfilled by Christ himself, but there are many for us to claim as our own. The purpose of this study is to help us to take hold of these promises and proclaim them over our lives. Read Hebrews 4:12 and write it here:

_____

What two words describe God's word _____ and _____. So far we have learned that all words can either be life giving or death giving BUT God's word is alive and it's powerful. (Hebrews 4:12 KJV) I want each of us to ask God to help us to be slow to speak and to filter our words through the truth and hope of God's word and his promises so we may speak life. Take a few moments now and ask Jesus for his wisdom and His truth to be revealed to you today. Read the following statement from John 1:1: "IN the beginning was the Word, and the Word was with God, and the Word was God." (John 1:1). This verse proves that the words contained in the bible, God's words are very powerful and are the very essence of who He is. So let's go to the beginning…….

Read Genesis 1:1-25 write any word or verse(s) that stick out to you.

_____

_____

_____

In the creation story, beginning with Genesis 1 each new day began with the words; "And God said." Genesis 1:3 NIV We know God said let there be light and there was light, God said separate the sea from dry land and it happened as He said, of course it did he is God. Now Reread verses 1-10 again. In verses 3, 6 &9 it is written God SAID and what he said happened. In verses 5,8 &10 it reads God called. First God creates then he defines it. God could have thought it, waved his hand, nodded his head, but he chose to speak to teach us that His words have creative power and because God also created man in His image (Genesis 1:27 KJV) and we too have this same power. Let's go back to Genesis at the creation story to reveal this truth. Read Genesis 2:19-20, write any verses or words that jump out at you.

God gave Adam a mouth to speak with and his first job was to name the creatures that God placed before him. In Genesis 2:20 it says God brought all the living creatures to Adam to name. And whatever the man called each creature that was its name. God gave Adam the power to name the things that crossed his path. We too are given the same power each new day, what words are you saying each day to yourself, others and the circumstances that cross your path?

When we think about our everyday life and the words we use without even thinking what words or phrases do you tend to say almost daily. Take time to write at least 5 down now.

_____

_____

Here are a few examples:

I love you, I am tired, work is so hard, I hate my boss, I am so impatient, My house is a mess, I'll never get this done, I have so much work to do, Have a good day.

I want you to circle the negative phrases you wrote and turn them into God's truth instead of saying, "I'm tired," we can say, "the Lord is renewing my strength, I will walk and not grow weary, I will run and not faint." (Isaiah 40:31 NIV). "I have so much work to do," becomes, "thank you Lord that you establish the works of my hands." (Psalm 90:17 NIV). I want you to take the negative words you wrote up or other ones you say and replace it with a scripture verse of God's truth. I want you to write those truths on a post it note or note card and tape it to something you look at everyday..a bathroom mirror, a closet. I used to put mine on my steering wheel and everytime I stopped at a red light I read it outloud, or on my kitchen sink window because I clean a whole lot of dishes. The point is to get those truths in front of you numerous times a day and SPEAK them out loud. Remember Adam didn't think of the names of the animals but called them out loud. I want you to go back to your list of everyday phrases and underline the positive ones.

Now take a positive phrase and give it power. For example, "I love you, you are the apple of God's eye (Psalm 17:8 NIV), he delights in you (Zephaniah 3:17 NIV).." "Good luck on your test," transforms into, "Lord, thank you that you are all knowing and you give me wisdom and knowledge." Good morning becomes, "This is the day the Lord has made; let us rejoice and be glad in it." Psalms 118:24 ESV Are you experiencing any change in mood or feeling when you added scripture to your words? I know I do, my spirit feels lifted and I have hope and joy rising up in me. Now add those verses to a note card and post them somewhere you look multiple times a day. I cannot stress enough the discipline of memorizing scripture. I want you to practice them each day. The more you practice scripture the more naturally it will flow from your mouth. You will notice soon, that you will stop yourself before saying something harmful because a life giving verse will come to your mind.

WEEK TWO

How are you doing with your scripture verses? If you haven't practiced, ask God now to give you a desire for memorizing his word. Ask him for ease in memorizing and thank him that he has given you the mind of Christ to help you.

Today we are going to see some examples of Proverbs 18:21 in action in the scriptures. Let's go back to God's word and see an example of the importance of speaking life giving words to the people God has put in our life.

Read Genesis 35:16-22, write anything the Holy Spirit impresses upon your heart below.

_____

_____

_____

In Genesis Chapter 35 beginning at verse 16 we come across the story of Rachel giving birth a second time. We know that Rachel had a hard time getting pregnant. She and her husband Jacob cried out to God for a child and God answered their prayers after many years with the birth of Joseph. But God is so good that he allowed Rachel to conceive and give birth again. But during this delivery Rachel was experiencing unbearable pain, we can imagine her in great distress and pain as the midwife says, "don't be afraid you have another son." (Genesis 35:17NLT)But Rachel in her deep agony of the moment and with her final breath names her son Ben-Oni; which means son of my trouble. Rachel made the mistake of naming her child based on her immediate struggle and pain, she was blinded by the pain and couldn't see the joy and blessing of another son. But Jacob, the boy's father, thankfully did and renamed him Benjamin which literally means son of my right hand. You see Jacob understood the power of blessing words from a father, he was so desperate to hear words of blessing and encouragement that he tricked his father Isaac into giving him the blessing over his brother (Genesis 27). Jacob knew the power his words would have in his son's life. He made sure they were words that brought him honor. He didn't want his son to walk around with the "trouble" label his whole life. He realized that yes he had a moment where he brought trouble to his mom but HE was not trouble. Just like Benjamin you may have put labels on yourself or others that did not come from your heavenly father. Maybe you put labels on yourself like, unorganized, stressed out, ugly, anxious. Or perhaps you've labeled other people, unmotivated, hyper, exhausting, lazy. These damaging labels need to stop. We need to begin to see ourselves and others as God our father sees us. Holy unto the Lord, redeemed, forgiven. Spend some time in prayer and ask the Holy Spirit to reveal a lie you have labeled yourself or someone else. Use the next page to make your list. Write your name or the person's name on the top, write the lies you have believed about yourself or someone else.

Name:	Name:
Lie	Truth
1.	1.
2.	2.
3.	3.
4.	4.
5.	5.

Let's go back to the book of Genesis with Adam and Eve, where it all went wrong. Slowly and intentionally read Genesis 3:1-11. If you're comfortable highlight or underline the phrases in your bible verses that stick out to you, otherwise write them below.

_____

_____

_____

The verse I want you to ponder is vs 11, "And He (God) said, "'WHO TOLD YOU THAT you were naked?" (Genesis 3:11 NLT) (emphasis mine) I ask you that same thing, who told you that you are weak, who told you that you aren't smart, who told you weren't loved, who told you that……… If it wasn't God it's not true. PERIOD. We don't get to define ourselves or others, God does. Adam and Eve walked freely and naked in a beautiful prepared garden WITH God. They felt no shame no embarrassment until that sneaky serpent whispered those lies to Eve…God doesn't want you to have, to know etc. What did Adam and Eve do, they hid. What lie are you hiding behind, or where do you see someone you love hiding behind a wrong label. I want you to take that previous page where you wrote the lie on one side and write the truth found in God's word on the other. I wrote some sample verses in the back of the book that might speak truth to your lie. Now carefully rip up the lie side and burn it!! Write those truths down and post them for memorization.

Beloved, in this age it is so easy for us to gossip, belittle and tear down ourselves and others with our words, we hide behind screens and, "call it as it is" or "as we see it." Please let us use our words to build up and not tear down, to heal and restore. We are a reflection of Jesus and our words were meant to bring healing and restoration to dry souls. Read Ephesians 4:29 NLT, "Don't use foul or abusive language. Let everything we say be good and helpful so that your words will be an encouragement to those who hear them."

Notice it said EVERYTHING we say be good and helpful, not some things. Not if a person deserves kind things spoken to them or if they say kind things to me. It doesn't say if your behavior is good then compliment yourself or others with a kind word, or good job. No, it says let everything you say be good so we and others can be encouraged…not beaten down and belittled. I have to admit I struggle with sarcasm, and however funny I may think it is or how much others laugh, I can assure you God is not laughing with me. He takes no pleasure in me tearing people down or myself. We are all His masterpieces, precious and honored in His sight. His ways are not our ways and His thoughts not our thoughts. BUT the power of the Holy spirit in us is present to help us align our thoughts and our ways to His perfection.

Proverbs 15:4 MSG translation states, "Kind words heal and help; cutting words wound and maim." Let's bring healing to ourselves and others. I want you to think of a person who could use a word of encouragement, write them a note and put a truth of God's word in it. Maybe the person who was on the top of that paper! Now get that note to that person ASAP..mail it or hand deliver, place it on their car..do it within 24 hours if possible.

WEEK THREE

Ok, I'm checking in…. Have you been practicing the verses you wrote down. Are you beginning to catch yourself mid hurtful word or thought and changing it to God's truth. That is my prayer for us all. I promise, the more you read, memorize and rehearse God's word over your life and the lives of those around you, you will begin to see hope rising in your heart and theirs. This discipline will soon become natural and more effortless. The last few days we have focused on our words towards people, we have read that our words can help lift and heal the hurting. Our words can shape the way someone views themselves and as Christ followers our words should be an encouragement and life giving, but can our words affect our circumstances?

We not only need to speak these life giving truth words to people but we have to speak them over our circumstances to bring the same hope, healing and restoration. Let's go back to God's word, in and of ourselves we have nothing profound to say, but God always does.

I want you to read Ezekiel 37, The Valley Of Dry Bones. Again please highlight or write below any words or thoughts the Holy Spirit impresses upon your spirit.

_____

_____

_____

This story is one of the most powerful scripture passages in my opinion. Can you imagine yourself among a bunch of lifeless, dry scattered bones? That is truly Death Valley. Now the teacher in me would like you to fill in the blanks the best you can (I gave you a word bank) We will go through them together as we continue our study.

Ezekiel 37: The valley of Dry Bones

1. We have to _____ the word of The Lord to the dry areas of our life.

2. Speaking God's word is a _____ act.

3. With God _____ is always alive

Word Bank

Hope; Continuous; Speak

Let's break this passage down and make it apply to our daily lives. However, if you want to be so bold as to stand in a graveyard and speak life to some dead bones, please let me know your results. I have learned not to put anything past God's power.

I want us first to see in verse 4 "Dry bones hear the word of the Lord!" Ezekiel 37:4CSB First, we have to <u>speak</u> the word of the Lord to the dry areas in our life (our relationships, children, jobs and health).

Look up Numbers 14:28 and write it below:

_____

I'll admit that verse leaves me speechless........I'm just going to let it linger there...read it aloud again then sit in silence for a full minute. God will do what hears coming out of our mouth. say, "I'm overweight" and pounds will start adding up on the scale over time. Say, "I'm fearfully and wonderfully made" Psalm 139:14 ESV and you will begin to glow with God's radiance. If you look back on your life can you see an example of something you repeatedly told yourself and now it is your reality? I can, and most of them were negative. The good news is we can change our words into God's truth and speak the victory God has in store for us.

In verse 7 Ezekiel says, "and as I was prophesying" Ezekiel 37:7 NIV. The second blank is, this is a <u>continuous</u> act. We need to continue to speak to our situations using God's word until life comes into us, until we begin to have hope again. Little by little our hope grows and we may experience glimpses of healing and restoration or complete restoration, to God be the Glory.

Read 2 Corinthians 5:7 and write it below.

_____

Our current circumstances aren't the end, it's not our permanent destination. Our reality is not God's viewpoint. We are passing through the valley of the shadow of death. There are mountain views ahead of us. For Jesus said, " all things are possible to him who believes" Mark 9:23 NKJV. Jesus again stated in Luke 18:27 NASB "the things which are impossible with men are possible with God."

The dry bones came together *slowly,* bone to bone, then tendons and flesh, but still no breath, no life so God commanded Ezekiel to keep prophesying. Changes don't always happen overnight. We must persevere through the trial and temptations while speaking the victories God has promised us.

In verse 11 God says, they say, "Our bones are dried up and our hope is gone; we are cut off." Ezekiel 37:11 NIV, basically this is Satan telling us or our thoughts saying there is no use, it's over this will never change. But the Sovereign Lord says, "My people, I am going to open your graves and bring you up from them" Ezekiel 37:12 NIV. Finally with God hope is always alive.

Take a few moments to meditate on the following verse from the book of Hebrews, "Faith is the assurance of things hoped for, the convictions of things not seen." Hebrews 11:1 ESV

We have assurance because God is faithful, it is not dependent upon us, our upbringing, nationality, where we live, our work ethic or education. It is however based on Christ and His finished work on the cross, and His work is finished! He is already seated next to the father in heaven. Resting, knowing His work is sufficient. He defeated every obstacle in your way. Our role is to agree with God. Read 2 Corinthians 1:20 below

"For no matter how many promises God has made, They are "yes" in Christ. And so through him the "Amen" is Spoken by US to the glory of God." (emphasis mine) 2 Corinthians 1:20 NIV

Our "job" is simply to take God at His word. Believe Him, trust him no matter how grim the situation or relationship. He is worthy to be trusted. It brings God much glory when we trust him and his promises are fulfilled in our lives. To Him be the Glory forever and ever.

Maybe you have heard the saying, "don't get your hopes up." Maybe growing up you heard that phrase from a parent not wanting you to get too excited in case things didn't work out the way you hoped for. I get it, as a parent you hate to see your kids disappointed but God's word says the exact opposite,

Read Proverbs 13:12 below. "Hope deferred makes the heart sick, but when the desire is fulfilled, it is a tree of life." Proverbs 13:12 AMPC

I want you to take a moment and write a desire you have in your heart, it may be a restored relationship, a job or career you desire, a spouse, for a child. A desire that pains your heart because it is not yet fulfilled.

_____

Once you have your desire write out a few promises from scripture that may speak to that situation. The scriptures don't have to be word for word but a general idea/ knowledge, you can write the exact verse later. You can reference the scriptures in the back of the book if you need help.

PROMISES

_____

_____

_____

_____

I want you now to write a letter to God pouring out your heart BUT I want you to remind God of His promises to you. You see God is faithful and he is trustworthy to fulfill his word. I wrote a sample letter that revolves around the theme of a child raised to know the Lord but has fallen away from God. You will find this sample letter in the back of the study.

So how do we keep our hopes up, we trust God at his word, at his promises we recite them over and over again until our spirit comes alive. Review the verses you have been working on now.

WEEK FOUR

If we want to move forward and not get stuck where we are, then we need to place our circumstances under the lense of God's truth. One of the saddest stories to me in all the bible is of the Israelites wandering in the desert for 40 yrs. God sent 12 spies in to see the land that he had promised to give to them. Read Numbers 13. They all saw the same thing, great huge fruit, beautiful land and giants. Out of the 12 spies only two saw the promise, the potential knowing the promise was theirs because God said it was. The other ten saw the obstacle, the giants. Numbers 13:33 KJV reads,"And there we saw the giants, the sons of Anak, which come of the giants; and we were in our own sight as grasshoppers, and so we were in their sight." Notice they saw themselves as grasshoppers, small, worthless and weak. The giants did not see them that way until they saw themselves that way. The scripture says God provoked fear in the nations because they knew God was with them (Numbers 22:3 NIV).If we want the victory God has already given us in Christ we must trust God at his word and not shrink back in fear. Caleb and Jacob saw the same giants as the other ten spies but they chose to believe God when He said he would give them this land, they focused on the fruit. Would they have to fight the enemy, YES but God promised victory. God promises us victory too, but it costs something, we too will have to fight the enemy, with the word of God to obtain the fruit. Read Ephesians 6:10-17. List the items we need to battle spiritual warfare:

_____

_____

_____

_____

Listen, if I'm in a true fight for my life, and an enemy is charging towards me ready to devour me, I don't think having a belt and shoes will do me nearly as much good as a sword? What is the sword? The very word of God. Can I remind you, we are in a battle, and it's against the devil, our adversary, and he does not want God's children living the abundant life Jesus promises us. (John 10:10)

Read James 3:4-6 CSB, " And consider the ships: Though very large and driven by fierce winds, they are guided by a very small rudder wherever the will of the pilot directs. So too, though the tongue is a small part of the body, it boasts great things. Consider how a small fire sets ablaze a large forest. And the tongue is a fire. The tongue, a world of unrighteousness, is placed among our members. It stains the whole body, sets the course of life on fire, and is itself set on fire by hell" James compares the tongue to a small rudder of a boat making a huge ship turn wherever the pilot chooses to go even through the winds and storm. Our words have the power to change the course of our life, our direction. When the storms of life come, sickness, financial struggle, trouble at school, work, difficult relationships, it's time to speak God's truth over our lives. The storms and struggles of life will come and continue to come but God in His word gives us the power to navigate through these storms and get to where he is leading us. Do you have your rudder (tongue) speaking on the power and promises of God? James goes on to say, "Can a fig tree produce olives or a grapevine produce figs? Neither can a saltwater spring yield fresh water" James 3:12 CSB. Beloved are your words salty or sweet, life releasing/resurrecting or death releasing/defeating? We can not simply state the reality we are in but must aim our rudder in the direction we want our life to take, and It's only found in the hope and promises of scripture.

Our struggles and difficult times were never meant to defeat us but to show us God's power.

Paul calls them, light momentary afflictions that are preparing for us an eternal weight of glory beyond all comparison. 2 Corinthians 4:17 ESV. We need to view them as light and momentary. We need to keep our focus on our all sufficient King and keep his word ever flowing from our mouth. We need to continually offer up a sacrifice of praise to our God (Hebrews 13:15 ESV). In the book of Acts we see Paul and Silas chained in prison for spreading the Good news. Read Acts 16:19-36. "It says at midnight (a dark hour) Paul and Silas prayed, and sang praises unto God:and the prisoners heard them." Acts 16:25 KJV With a violent earthquake the chains around them were broken and the prison walls crumbled, setting them free and the prisoners and guards. Our never ending praise in the most dire of circumstances can set not only us free but those who hear us. This cannot be a silent act, the enemy cannot read our thoughts but at the name of Jesus he must eventually retreat. For the remainder of today I want you to find a partner or break into small groups or if you are doing the study alone, phone a trusted friend and discuss how you have seen God move as you have implemented His word in your life. Or admit your struggle. Pray for one another. James 5:16 NASB says, "Confess your trespasses to one another, and pray for one another, that you may be healed. The effective, fervent prayer of a righteous man avails much."

WEEK FIVE

I want to end our study in Luke 1: 5-20 . Please take time to read it now, again right any thoughts or key ideas that speak to you personally.

_____

_____

_____

_____

_____

Now I want you to fill in the blanks the best you can using the word bank...

Birth of John the baptist foretold

Luke 1 Birth of John the Baptist Foretold

1. God hears our _____.

2. Our _____ doesn't abort the _____.

3. _____ _____ the unbelief.

4. God will bring the promise to pass in His perfect _____.

(sometimes promises are meant for future generations)

Word Bank: timing; zip up; prayers; promise, doubt;

When the birth of John the Baptist is foretold to Zechariah, a priest, an angel of the Lord appears to Zechariah and he says, "don't be afraid Zechariah your prayer has been heard. Your wife Elizabeth will bear you a son, and you are to call him John." (Luke 1:13). Be assured dear one God has heard your prayer. (first blank). We don't know how long Zechariah has been praying for this child, but I love how God has already named him...he doesn't even exist yet! Now being the great man of faith Zechariah was, he looks at the situation, knowing the facts, Elizabeth is old, we have tried so long, I have prayed so much. Zechariah asks the angel in verse 18 "How can I be sure of this? I am an old man and my wife is well along in years." Luke 1:18 NIV Basically Zechariah says, this is absurd, prove it… What Gabriel speaks is profound, he says, Look at verse 20 again. " I have been sent to you to tell you this good news. And now you will be silent and not be able to speak until the day this happens, BECAUSE YOU DID NOT BELIEVE MY WORDS, WHICH WILL COME TRUE AT THEIR PROPER TIME." Luke 1:20 NIV (emphasis mine). Notice the angel said, "it will come true." Our second blanks are Our doubt doesn't abort God's promise. The Lord caused Zechariah to be silent because he didn't believe the truth, his words could be destructive because in his heart he didn't believe. I say this with so much love, you may need to just keep your mouth closed. If your heart doesn't believe it, go to God but don't speak unbelief, don't let it come out. Our third blanks are to zip up the unbelief. God will fulfil his promises, He is faithful. "God is not human, that he should lie, not a human being, that he should change his mind. Does he speak and then not act? Does he promise and not fulfill?" Numbers 23:19 NIV. Beloved, God will fulfil his promise in His perfect timing. (our final blank). Be like Mary, the mother of Jesus when she heard the shocking news that she would be having a baby without being intimate with a man, and not any baby but God himself, she said, "Be it unto me as you have said." Luke 1:38 KJV. When Elizabeth, the mother of John the Baptist, saw Mary with child she exclaimed, "Blessed is she who has believed that the Lord would fulfil his promise to her!" Luke 1:45 NIV. I am going to be honest, when I first came to be a follower of Jesus, the very first words I heard the Lord speak to me were, "shut your mouth" I was so negative, such a grumbler and God in his great love for me had to tell me to keep my mouth closed from speaking such doubt and negativity into my life. If I was going to walk with him and expect my life to be any different, then my words needed to be different, life giving! God wants us to pour our hearts out to him but more importantly he wants us to move forward in faith.

It is imperative that we begin to renew our minds with the truth of God's word. God is the voice of truth, and everything that does not line up with the truth found in God's word is a lie from our adversary the devil. Read 2 Corinthians 10:5 and write it below.

_____

_____

_____

If our thoughts don't line up with God's truth either will our words. It is going to be hard, it will take discipline but the more we recite out loud God's truth the more we will see it bearing fruit in our lives and the lives around us. We must renew our mind with God's truth and just as importantly speak that truth into our lives and the lives around us, so that it is God's voice that shapes us, molds us and changes us into the people he created us to be. Even though our study is over, the study of God's word never ends, study Jesus, sit with him. Allow Him to search your heart, he is gentle and compassionate. HE who began a good work in you will complete it. Run to him and soak in his promises they will be life for your soul.

"So commit yourselves wholeheartedly to these words of mine, tie them to your hands and wear them on your forehead as reminders. Teach them to your children and talk about them when you are at home and when you are on the road, when you are going to bed and when you are getting up." Deuteronomy 11:18-19 NLT

EXAMPLE PRAYER

Lord, I lift _____ up to you. He has been believing the lie that it is more important to please friends than you. I repent of any negative thought or word that I may have said to make him believe that you are not a friend of sinners. Lord purify my heart and help me to see him through your eyes of love, compassion and mercy. Give me words to encourage and give him hope that you do in fact call him friend (John 15:13 CSB). Father I come now boldly to the throne room of Grace and ask that you would give_____ a desire to please you O' Lord; and not try to please man, for it is you who test his heart. (1 Thessalonians 2:4 ESV), Thank you that you cleanse him from all unrighteousness (1 John 1:9 CSB).Father you said that your Spirit who is on me and your words that you have put in my mouth will not depart from me or the mouth of my children and their descendants from this time on and forever. (Isaiah 59:21 NIV) so Lord I praise you for putting a new song in his mouth, a hymn of praise to you O God (Psalm 40:3 CSB) I ask that _____ would not follow the crowd in doing wrong (Exodus 23:2 NIV) but that he would walk with the wise so that he may be wise (proverbs 13:20 CSB). Lord you said, the beginning of wisdom is the fear of the Lord, so I thank you for giving _____ a holy fear of you and your great name. Help him to be a friend to all who fear you, to all those who keep your precepts (Psalm 119:63 CSB). I pray this in Jesus' mighty name . AMEN

SCRIPTURE VERSES

FAMILY/RELATIONSHIPS

"As for me and my house, we will serve the Lord" Joshua 24:15 NLT

"Her children rise up and call her blessed; her husband also, and he praises her." Proverbs 31:28 CSB

"He gives the barren woman a home, making her the joyous mother of children. Praise the Lord" Psalm 119:9 ESV

"How wonderful and pleasant it is when brothers live together in unity." Psalm 133:1 NLT

"As a father has compassion on his children, so the Lord has compassion on those who fear him." Psalm 103:13 CSB

"Train up a child in the way he should go: and when he is old, he will not depart from it." Proverbs 22:6 KJV

"Husbands love your wives, and be not bitter against them." Colossians 3:19 KJV

"Wives submit to your own husband, as to the Lord." Ephesians 5:22 ESV

"Father's, do not provoke your children to anger, but bring them up in the discipline and instruction of the Lord." Ephesians 6:4 ESV

FINANCES/LACK

"But my God shall supply all your needs according to his riches in glory by Christ Jesus." Philippians 4:19 KJV

"When the Lord God blesses you as He has promised you, then you will lend to many nations, but you will not borrow; and you will rule over many nations, but they will not rule over you." Deuteronomy 15:6

"And my God will supply every need of yours according to his riches in glory in Christ Jesus." Philippians 4:19 ESV

MIND/ANXIETY

"I am leaving you with a gift-peace of mind and heart. And the peace I give is a gift the world cannot give. So don't be troubled or afraid." John 14:27 NLT

"Casting down imaginations, and every high thing that exalteth itself against the knowledge of God, and bringing into captivity every thought to the obedience of Christ." 2 Corinthians 10:5 KJV

"Do not be anxious about anything, but in everything by prayer and supplication with thanksgiving let your request be known to God. And the peace of God will, which surpasses all understanding will guard your hearts and mind in Christ Jesus." Philippians 4:6-7 ESV

"For who has known the Lord's mind, that he may instruct him? But we have the mind of Christ." 1 Corinthians 2:16 CSB

"For God did not give us a spirit of timidity or cowardice or fear, but {He has given us a spirit} of power and of love and of sound judgment and personal discipline {abilities resulting in a calm, well-balanced mind and self-control}. 2 Timothy 1:7 AMP

Casting all your cares on him, because he cares for you. 1 Peter 5:7 ESV

"I have said these things to you, that in me you may have peace, in the world you will have tribulation. But take heart; I have overcome the world." John 16:33 ESV

"Now may the Lord of peace himself give you peace at all times in every way. The Lord be with youall." 2 Thessalonians 3:16 ESV

"You keep him in perfect peace whose mind is stayed on you, because he trusts in you." Isaiah 26:3 ESV

"Peace I leave with you; my peace I give to you. Not as the world gives do I give to you. Let not your hearts be troubled, neither let them be afraid." John 14:27

"And be not conformed to this world; but be ye transformed by the renewing of your mind, that ye may prove what is that good, and acceptable,and perfect, will of God." Romans 12:2 KJV

HEALTH

"But he was pierced for our transgressions, he was crushed for our iniquities; the punishment that brought us peace was on him, and by his wounds we are healed" Isaiah 53:5 NIV

"And the prayer offered in faith will make the sick person well; the Lord will raise them up. If they have sinned, they will be forgiven." James 5:15 NIV

"He himself bore our sins in his body on the cross, so that we might die to sins and live for righteousness; by his wounds you have been healed." 1 Peter 2:24 NIV

"He forgives all my sins and heals all my diseases." Psalm 103:3 NLT

"He heals the broken hearted and binds up their wounds." Psalm 147:3 NIV

"Nevertheless, I will bring health and healing to it; I will heal my people and will let them enjoy abundant peace and security." Jeremiah 33:6 NIV

Depression/joy

"These things I have spoken to you, that my joy may remain in you, and that your joy might be full." John 5:11 KJV

"You make known to me the path of life; in your presence is fullness of joy ; at your right hand are pleasures forevermore." Psalm 16:11 NIV

"This is the day the Lord has made, let us rejoice and be glad in it." Psalm 118:24 NIV

"For you shall go out in joy and be led forth in peace; the mountains and the hills before you shall break forth into singing, and all the trees of the field shall clap their hands." Isaiah 55:12 ESV

"I sought the Lord and he answered me and delivered me from all my fears." psalm 34:4 ESV

Printed in the United States
By Bookmasters